CANON EOS R5 MARK II- QUICK & CONCISE GUIDE

Modes, Shooting & Setting Processes (Photographer's Quick-Guide Series)

Sam Addy

Table of Contents

Overview of the Canon EOS R5 Mark II

The Canon EOS R5 Mark II is a cutting-edge full-frame mirrorless camera that builds upon the success of its predecessor, the EOS R5. Designed for professional photographers and videographers, it delivers unparalleled imaging performance, enhanced video capabilities, and improved autofocus precision. With its advanced sensor technology, high-speed processing, and refined ergonomics, the EOS R5 Mark II pushes the boundaries of mirrorless camera innovation.

Key Features at a Glance:

- Advanced Full-Frame CMOS Sensor – Delivers superior image resolution, dynamic range, and low-light performance.
- Enhanced Dual Pixel Autofocus II – Faster, more accurate subject tracking, including improved eye, face, and animal detection.
- 8K and 4K Video Recording – Supports high-resolution recording with enhanced heat management for longer shooting durations.
- High-Speed Continuous Shooting – Up to 30 fps with electronic shutter and 12 fps with the mechanical shutter.
- Upgraded Image Stabilization – Advanced In-Body Image Stabilization (IBIS) for sharper handheld shots.
- New AI-Based Subject Recognition – Improves autofocus tracking for a wide range of subjects, including vehicles, birds, and more.
- Dual Memory Card Slots – Supports CFexpress Type B and SD UHS-II cards for flexible storage options.
- Enhanced Connectivity – Faster Wi-Fi 6, Bluetooth 5.0, and USB-C 3.2 for seamless data transfer and remote control.
- Improved Weather Sealing – More durable construction for professional use in extreme conditions.

Designed for Professionals and Enthusiasts

The EOS R5 Mark II is engineered for photographers and videographers who demand high performance in every shooting scenario. Whether capturing high-resolution stills, fast-action sports, cinematic video, or wildlife photography, the camera delivers exceptional results with its refined sensor and autofocus system.

Overview of the Canon EOS R5 Mark II

With a lightweight yet durable magnesium alloy body, an intuitive control layout, and a high-resolution articulating touchscreen, it offers a seamless shooting experience. The updated heat dissipation system ensures prolonged 8K recording, making it a go-to choice for filmmakers and content creators who require uncompromised video quality.

A Step Forward in Mirrorless Innovation

The Canon EOS R5 Mark II represents a significant leap in mirrorless technology, blending speed, precision, and versatility to meet the demands of modern imaging professionals. Whether in the studio or on location, this camera ensures outstanding quality, reliability, and creative freedom.

Who is this Guide for?

This guide is for anyone who wants to master the Canon EOS R5 Mark II, whether you're a beginner or an experienced photographer. It's designed to help you understand, set up, and use the camera effectively for photography and video.

Who Will Benefit from This Guide?

- Beginners – If you're new to mirrorless cameras, this guide will walk you through the basics in a simple and easy-to-follow way.
- Enthusiasts – If you enjoy photography as a hobby and want to improve your skills, you'll find helpful tips on camera settings and creative shooting techniques.
- Professional Photographers – If you shoot portraits, landscapes, sports, or wildlife, this guide will help you maximize the camera's advanced features.
- Videographers and Filmmakers – If you're looking to record 8K or 4K high-quality videos, you'll learn how to optimize settings for professional results.
- Content Creators – If you create videos for YouTube, vlogging, or social media, this guide covers everything from autofocus to wireless file transfers.

No matter your skill level, this guide will help you unlock the full potential of your Canon EOS R5 Mark II and take your photography and videography to the next level.

CANON EOS R100 SPOT

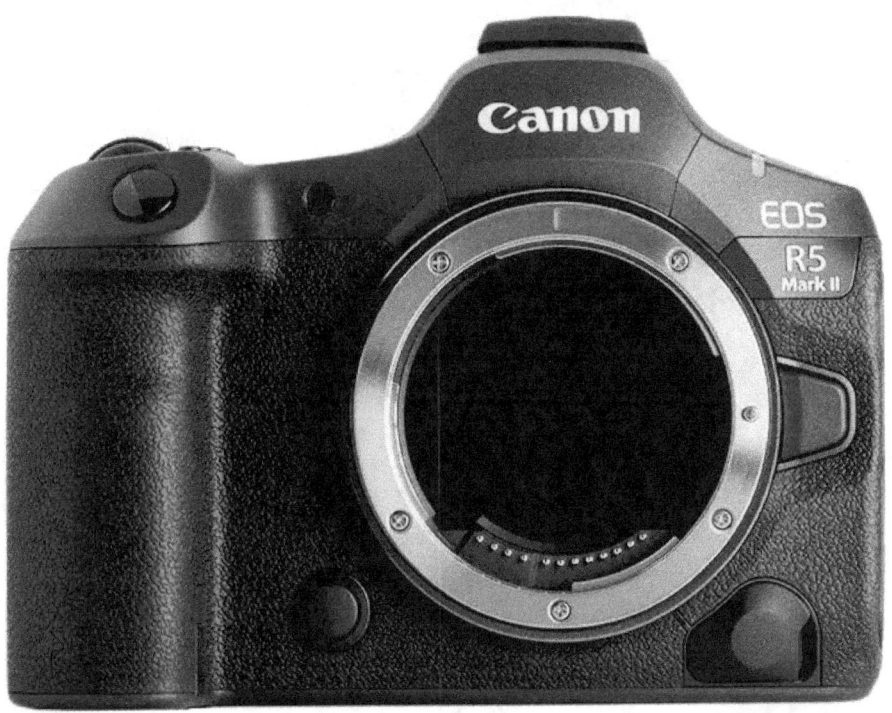

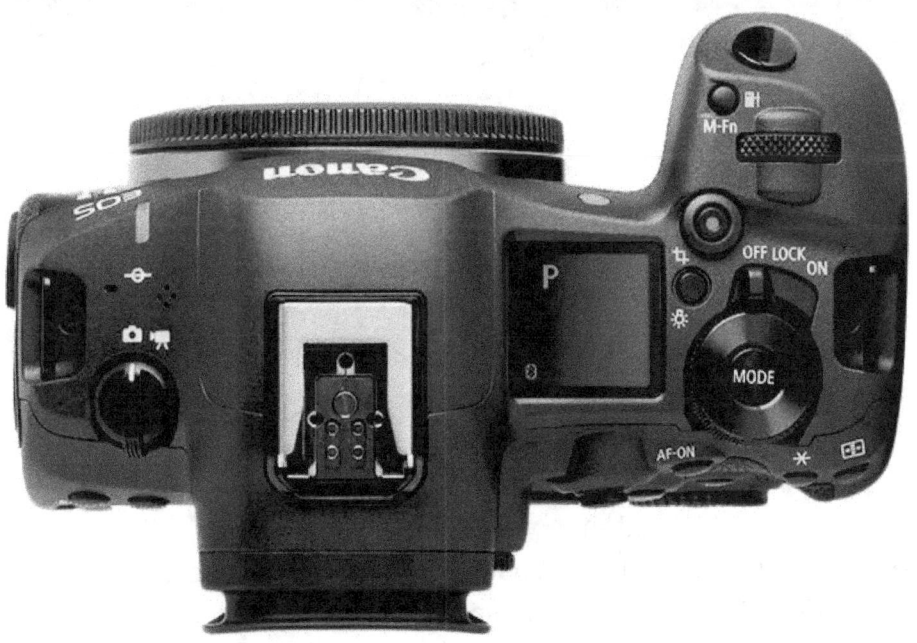

GET FAMILIARIZE WITH PARTS

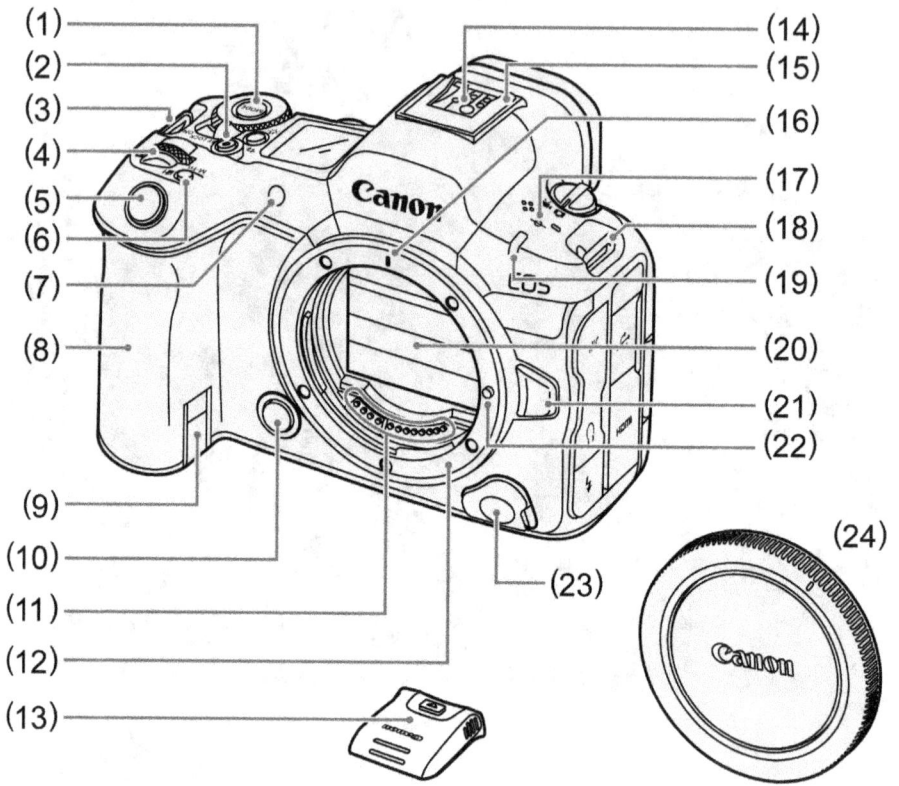

1. MODE Button
   - Description: This button allows you to switch between different shooting modes such as Manual (M), Aperture Priority (Av), Shutter Priority (TV), and Auto.
   - Mode of Operation: Press the button and rotate the Main Dial to select the desired shooting mode.
   - Usage: Use this to quickly change between photo and video shooting modes based on your shooting needs.

2. Movie Shooting Button
   - Description: A dedicated button for recording videos.
   - Mode of Operation: Press once to start recording and again to stop.
   - Usage: Quickly switch to video recording without changing modes manually.

GET FAMILIARIZE WITH PARTS

3. Strap Mount
- Description: A slot on both camera sides to attach a neck or wrist strap.
- Mode of Operation: Thread the strap through the mount and secure it.
- Usage: Ensures the camera is securely carried and prevents accidental drops.

4. Main Dial
- Description: A rotating dial is used to adjust camera settings.
- Mode of Operation: Turn to change parameters like shutter speed, aperture, or menu navigation.
- Usage: Quickly adjust settings while shooting without navigating through the menu.

5. Shutter Button
- Description: The main button is used to capture photos.
- Mode of Operation: Half-press to autofocus, full-press to take a photo.
- Usage: Essential for shooting photos with precise focus and timing.

6. Multi-function/FTP Server Image Transfer Button
- Description: A button used to access multiple camera functions, including image transfer via FTP.
- Mode of Operation: Press to access assigned functions or initiate FTP transfer.
- Usage: Useful for professional photographers who need to send images directly to a server.

7. Self-Timer Lamp/AF-Assist Beam
- Description: A small LED that indicates when the self-timer is active or assists with autofocus in low light.
- Mode of Operation: Lights up when the self-timer is active; projects a beam to assist AF in the dark.
- Usage: Helps with autofocus in dim environments and ensures subjects know when a timer shot is being taken.

8. Grip (Battery Compartment)
- Description: The camera's ergonomic grip that houses the battery.
- Mode of Operation: Provides a comfortable handhold and access to the battery slot.
- Usage: Ensures stability when shooting and allows battery replacement.

9. DC Coupler Cord Hole
- Description: A port for an external power source.
- Mode of Operation: Connects a DC coupler for extended shooting.
- Usage: Ideal for studio or time-lapse photography requiring continuous power.

10. Depth-of-Field Preview Button
- Description: A button that lets you preview how much of your image will be in focus.
- Mode of Operation: Press to see the effect of the selected aperture before taking the shot.
- Usage: Helps photographers adjust the aperture for better focus control.

11. Contacts
- Description: Electronic connectors between the camera and lens.
- Mode of Operation: Enables communication between the camera and lens.
- Usage: Ensures lens autofocus, stabilization, and aperture control function properly.

12. Lens Mount
- Description: The circular metal ring where the lens attaches.
- Mode of Operation: Align the lens and rotate it until it clicks.
- Usage: Allows RF-mount lenses and adapters for other lens types.

13. Shoe Cover
- Description: A protective cover for the camera's hot shoe.
- Mode of Operation: Slide the cover off to expose the Multi-function Shoe.
- Usage: Protects the hot shoe from dust and damage when not in use.

14. Flash Sync Contacts
- Description: Electrical contacts in the multi-function shoe for external flashes.
- Mode of Operation: Transmits signals to external flashes for synchronization.
- Usage: Enables studio flash triggers and external Speedlite.

15. Multi-function Shoe
- Description: An upgraded hot shoe supporting external accessories like microphones, flashes, and wireless transmitters.
- Mode of Operation: Slide compatible accessories into the shoe for direct connection.
- Usage: Ideal for video creators who need external audio or lighting.

16. RF Lens Mount Index
- Description: A red dot on the lens mount aligns RF lenses.
- Mode of Operation: Match the red dot on the lens with the red dot on the mount and twist to secure.
- Usage: Ensures proper lens attachment without misalignment.

17. Focal Plane Mark
- Description: A small marking that indicates the exact sensor plane inside the camera.
- Mode of Operation: Used for precise manual focus and measurements.
- Usage: Helps when measuring focus distance for macro or scientific photography.

18. Second Strap Mount
- Description: A slot on both camera sides to attach a neck or wrist strap.
- Mode of Operation: Thread the strap through the mount and secure it.
- Usage: Ensures the camera is securely carried and prevents accidental drops.

19. Tally Lamp
- Description: An indicator light that shows when video recording is active.

Mode of Operation: Lights up during video recording.

- Usage: Helps on-camera subjects know when recording is in progress.

20. Shutter Curtain/Image Sensor
- Description: The internal shutter controls exposure; the sensor captures images.
- Mode of Operation: The shutter opens to expose the sensor when capturing an image.
- Usage: Essential for controlling exposure and capturing light.

21. Lens Release Button
- Description: A button detaches the lens from the camera body.
- Mode of Operation: Press and twist the lens counterclockwise to remove it.
- Usage: Allows switching between different lenses.

22. Lens Lock Pin
- Description: A small locking mechanism that secures the lens in place.
- Mode of Operation: Clicks into place when the lens is mounted correctly.
- Usage: Prevents the lens from falling off accidentally.

23. Remote Control Terminal
- Description: A port for connecting wired remote shutter releases.
- Mode of Operation: Plug in a remote trigger to operate the shutter without touching the camera.
- Usage: Useful for long exposures, astrophotography, or self-portraits.

24. Body Cap
- Description: A protective cap for the camera mount.
- Mode of Operation: Twist onto the mount when no lens is attached.
- Usage: Protects the camera's sensor and contacts from dust and damage when a lens is not attached.

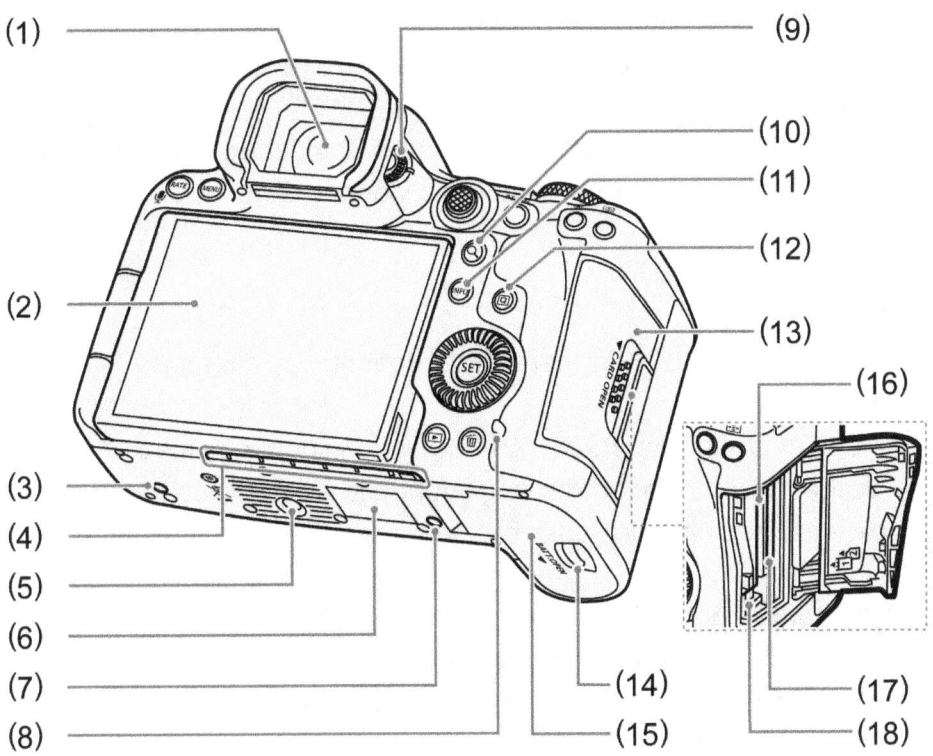

(1) (9) (10) (11) (12) (13) (16) (2) (3) (4) (5) (6) (7) (8) (14) (15) (17) (18)

1. LCD Panel
- Description: A high-resolution touchscreen display for live view, settings, playback, and touch controls.
- Mode of Operation: Can be tilted/swiveled for different shooting angles and used for touch autofocus, menu navigation, and image playback.
- Usage: Essential for reviewing photos, composing shots, adjusting settings, and navigating the menu with ease.

2. Eyecup
- Description: A soft rubber attachment surrounds the electronic viewfinder (EVF).
- Mode of Operation: Reduces glare and provides a comfortable view through the electronic viewfinder.
- Usage: Helps block out external light for better visibility, especially in bright environments.

3. Speaker

- Description: A small built-in speaker for playing back audio from video recordings.
- Mode of Operation: Automatically activates during video playback.
- Usage: Allows quick review of video sound without external headphones.

4. Microphone

- Description: A built-in stereo microphone for capturing in-camera audio.
- Mode of Operation: Records sound when shooting videos.
- Usage: Useful for recording general ambient sounds, though external microphones offer better quality.

5. Still Photo Shooting/Movie Recording Switch

- Description: A switch that toggles between photo and video modes.
- Mode of Operation: Slide to switch between modes; the mode is displayed on the LCD panel.
- Usage: Quickly changes the camera's function from stills to video recording.

6. Terminal Cover

- Description: A protective cover for various input/output ports.
- Mode of Operation: Open to access ports and close to protect against dust.
- Usage: Helps prevent damage and dust accumulation in critical connection ports.

7. External Microphone IN Terminal

- Description: A 3.5mm input jack for external microphones.
- Mode of Operation: Plug in a microphone to improve audio quality during video recording.
- Usage: Useful for vloggers, filmmakers, and interviews where clear audio is necessary.

8. Digital Terminal
- Description: A USB-C port for data transfer, tethered shooting, and charging.
- Mode of Operation: Connect the camera to a computer or external storage device.
- Usage: Allows image transfer, firmware updates, or remote shooting via software.

9. Exhaust Vent
- Description: A small vent to dissipate heat from internal components.
- Mode of Operation: Works automatically to prevent overheating during extended use.
- Usage: Especially important when recording high-resolution video for long durations.

10. Headphone Terminal
- Description: A 3.5mm audio output for connecting headphones.
- Mode of Operation: Plug in headphones to monitor audio while recording videos.
- Usage: Essential for professional video production where audio quality is critical.

11. HDMI OUT Terminal
- Description: A port for outputting video and images to an external monitor.
- Mode of Operation: Connect an HDMI cable to an external display or recorder.
- Usage: Useful for monitoring video in real-time on larger screens or external recording devices.

12. Sync Terminal
- Description: A PC sync port for connecting external flash systems.
- Mode of Operation: Triggers external flashes when using off-camera lighting setups.
- Usage: Essential for studio photography with strobe lights.

13. LCD Panel Info Switching/Illumination/Cropping Button
- Description: A multi-function button to adjust LCD display settings.
- Mode of Operation: Press to switch between different display modes or turn on backlight illumination.
- Usage: Helps customize the LCD view for different lighting conditions.

14. Power/Multi-Function Lock Switch
- Description: The main power switch with an additional lock function.
- Mode of Operation: Rotate to turn the camera on/off or lock specific controls.
- Usage: Prevents accidental setting changes during shooting.

15. Quick Control Dial 2
- Description: A secondary control dial for navigating menus and adjusting settings.
- Mode of Operation: Rotate to change settings quickly.
- Usage: Helps in fast exposure and menu adjustments.

16. AE Lock Button
- Description: Locks the current exposure settings.
- Mode of Operation: Press to lock exposure while recomposing a shot.
- Usage: Useful in high-contrast scenes where auto exposure may not be ideal.

17. AF Point Selection Button
- Description: Allows you to choose a focus point manually.
- Mode of Operation: Press and use the multi-controller or touchscreen to select a focus point.
- Usage: Helps in precise focusing for creative compositions.

18. AF Start Button
- Description: Initiates autofocus independently of the shutter button.
- Mode of Operation: Press to engage autofocus.
- Usage: Useful for back-button focusing, giving more control over focus adjustments.

19. Multi-Controller (Can Also Be Pressed Straight In)
- Description: A joystick-style controller used for navigating menus and selecting focus points.
- Mode of Operation: Move in multiple directions or press straight in.
- Usage: Speeds up menu navigation and focus point selection.

20. Quick Control Dial 1
- Description: The main control wheel used for adjusting settings.
- Mode of Operation: Rotate to change values like shutter speed or aperture.
- Usage: Essential for quick exposure adjustments while shooting.

21. Set Button
- Description: Confirms selections in the menu system.
- Mode of Operation: Press to confirm a setting or execute a function.
- Usage: Works with menu navigation, exposure adjustments, and custom functions.

22. Erase Button
- Description: Allows deletion of selected images.
- Mode of Operation: Press to delete photos/videos from the memory card.
- Usage: Helps in removing unwanted shots on the go.

23. Playback Button
- Description: Used to review photos and videos stored on the memory card.
- Mode of Operation: Press to enter playback mode.
- Usage: Allows for reviewing and managing images quickly.

24. Menu Button
- Description: Opens the camera's main menu system.
- Mode of Operation: Press to access settings and configurations.
- Usage: Used for adjusting camera settings, custom functions, and preferences.

25. Rating/Voice Memo Button
- Description: Adds star ratings or voice notes to images.
- Mode of Operation: Press to rate an image or record a short voice memo.
- Usage: Useful for sorting and annotating images quickly.

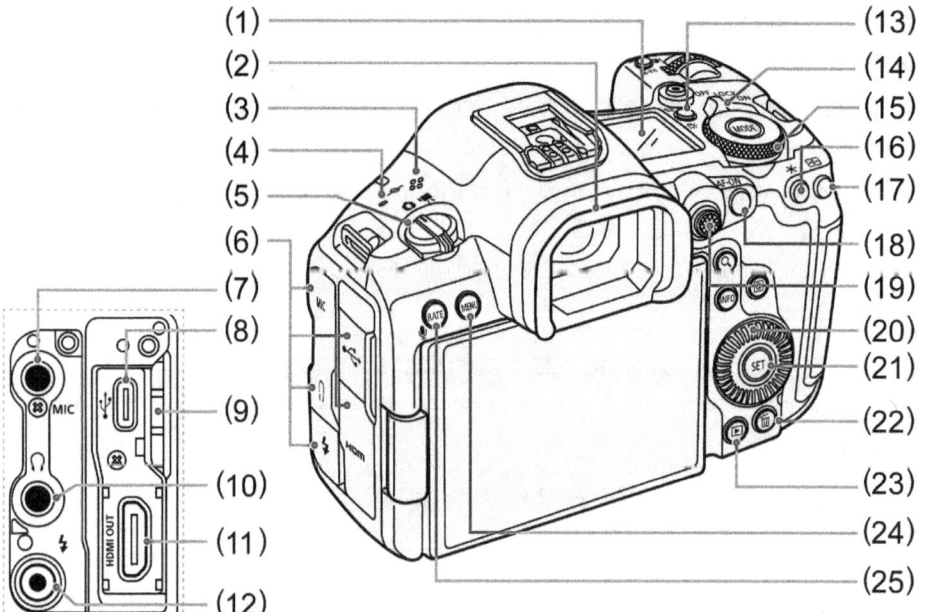

1. Viewfinder Eyepiece
- Description: The electronic viewfinder (EVF) window where you compose shots.
- Mode of Operation: Look through the EVF to see a live scene preview with exposure settings applied.
- Usage: Helps in bright outdoor conditions where the LCD screen may be difficult to see.

2. Screen
- Description: A high-resolution, articulating LCD touchscreen.
- Mode of Operation: Can be tilted/swiveled for different angles, and used for touch autofocus, menu navigation, and playback.
- Usage: Useful for low/high-angle shots, vlogging, and reviewing images/videos.

3. Accessory Positioning Hole
- Description: A small hole designed to securely mount accessories like grips and battery packs.
- Mode of Operation: Accessories align with this hole for stability.
- Usage: Ensures proper attachment of external accessories without slipping.

4. Intake Vent
- Description: A ventilation opening that allows cooling air to enter the camera.
- Mode of Operation: Works passively to prevent overheating during extended use.
- Usage: Important when shooting long-duration 8K/4K video.

5. Tripod Socket
- Description: A standard 1/4-inch metal thread for mounting the camera on a tripod or gimbal.
- Mode of Operation: Screw a tripod plate into the socket.
- Usage: Essential for stable photography and videography, especially for long exposures and time-lapses.

6. Serial Number (Body Number)
- Description: The unique identification number for the camera.
- Mode of Operation: Used for warranty, registration, and tracking.
- Usage: Needed for product registration, repairs, and warranty claims.

7. Accessory Positioning Hole
- Description: A small hole designed to securely mount accessories like grips and battery packs.
- Mode of Operation: Accessories align with this hole for stability.
- Usage: Ensures proper attachment of external accessories without slipping.

8. Access Lamp
- Description: A small LED indicator that lights up when the camera is reading/writing data to the memory card.
- Mode of Operation: Glows or blinks while saving or transferring files.
- Usage: Helps prevent accidental data corruption—never remove the memory card while the lamp is on.

9. Dioptric Adjustment Knob
- Description: A small wheel next to the viewfinder that adjusts the focus of the EVF to match your eyesight.
- Mode of Operation: Rotate until the viewfinder display looks sharp.
- Usage: Ideal for users with glasses or vision differences.

10. Magnify/Reduce Button
- Description: A button used for zooming in or out on images and menus.
- Mode of Operation: Press to enlarge or shrink playback images.
- Usage: Helps in checking image sharpness and fine details during playback.

11. Info Button
- Description: Toggles between different display modes on the LCD screen and viewfinder.
- Mode of Operation: Press to cycle through histogram, shooting settings, or no-display mode.
- Usage: Helps customize the screen layout based on shooting needs.

12. Quick Control Button
- Description: Opens the Quick Control menu for fast access to key settings.
- Mode of Operation: Press to adjust settings like ISO, shutter speed, and focus mode without opening the full menu.
- Usage: Saves time by allowing quick adjustments on the fly.

13. Card Slot Cover
- Description: A protective cover that shields the memory card slots.
- Mode of Operation: Slide to open and insert/remove memory cards.
- Usage: Protects memory cards from dust, moisture, and damage.

14. Battery Compartment Cover Lock
- Description: A small locking mechanism that secures the battery compartment.
- Mode of Operation: Slide or press to unlock before opening the battery compartment.
- Usage: Prevents accidental battery ejection.

15. Battery Compartment Cover
- Description: A hinged cover that encloses the battery.
- Mode of Operation: Opens when the cover lock is released.
- Usage: Protects the battery from dust and accidental removal.

16. Card Slot 1
- Description: The primary memory card slot, supporting CFexpress Type B cards.
- Mode of Operation: Insert the memory card until it clicks into place.
- Usage: CFexpress cards enable high-speed data writing, essential for 8K RAW video recording.

17. Card Slot 2
- Description: A secondary memory card slot supporting SD UHS-II cards.
- Mode of Operation: Works alongside Card Slot 1, offering backup storage or different file formats.
- Usage: Allows dual-card recording for redundancy or separate RAW/JPEG storage.

18. Card Eject Button
- Description: A small button next to each card slot used to eject memory cards.
- Mode of Operation: Press the button to release and remove the card.
- Usage: Ensures safe removal of memory cards without damage.

Understand Camera Modes

The Canon EOS R5 Mark II offers multiple shooting modes to suit different photography styles and levels of expertise. Whether you're a beginner looking for automatic assistance or a professional wanting full manual control, understanding these modes will help you get the best results.

This section will break down each mode, explaining when and how to use it effectively.

Auto Mode (Green Square Mode):

Let the Camera Do the Work

- In Auto Mode, the camera automatically adjusts settings such as shutter speed, aperture, ISO, and focus.
- Perfect for situations where you just want to point and shoot without worrying about technical details.
- The camera also uses Scene Recognition to optimize settings for landscapes, portraits, or night scenes.

While this mode is convenient, it limits your creative control. If you want more flexibility, try Program (P) Mode instead.

Scene Modes – Optimized for Different Situations

The Canon EOS R5 Mark II includes special Scene Modes that optimize settings for specific conditions:

- Portrait Mode – Softens the background (shallow depth of field) to make the subject stand out.
- Landscape Mode – Uses a small aperture for sharp focus across the entire scene.
- Sports Mode – Increases shutter speed for capturing fast-moving subjects.
- Night Portrait Mode – Balances flash and exposure for clear nighttime portraits.
- Macro Mode – Adjusts focus and aperture for close-up shots.

Scene modes are useful for beginners, but if you want more creative control, try Aperture Priority (Av) or Shutter Priority (Tv) modes.

Understand Camera Modes

Program Mode (P) – Semi-Automatic with More Control

- In Program Mode, the camera automatically sets shutter speed and aperture, but you can adjust other settings like ISO, white balance, and exposure compensation.
- This mode is a good step up from Auto Mode, giving you more flexibility while still letting the camera handle the exposure.

Use Exposure Compensation (by turning the main dial) to make your photos brighter or darker.

Shutter Priority Mode (Tv) – Controlling Motion

- In Shutter Priority (Tv) Mode, you control the shutter speed, and the camera adjusts the aperture automatically.
- Use fast shutter speeds (1/1000s or higher) to freeze motion (e.g., sports, wildlife, or action shots).
- Use slow shutter speeds (1/30s or lower) to create motion blur (e.g., waterfalls, light trails, or low-light scenes).

When using slow shutter speeds, use a tripod to avoid camera shake.

Aperture Priority Mode (Av) – Controlling Depth of Field

- In Aperture Priority (Av) Mode, you control the aperture (f-number) while the camera adjusts the shutter speed automatically.
- A low f-number (f/1.8 - f/2.8) creates a blurry background (good for portraits).
- A high f-number (f/8 - f/16) keeps everything focused (great for landscapes).

A wider aperture (low f-number) lets in more light, which is helpful in low-light situations.

Manual Mode (M) – Full Creative Control

- In Manual Mode, you manually set the shutter speed, aperture, and ISO.
- Best for challenging lighting conditions, creative photography, and long-exposure shots.
- You can adjust settings based on the Exposure Meter to get the correct brightness.

Bulb Mode (B) – Extra-Long Exposures

- Bulb Mode lets you keep the shutter open for as long as you hold the button (or use a remote trigger).
- Ideal for exposures longer than 30 seconds when capturing night skies, light trails, or smooth water.

Use a tripod and a remote shutter release to prevent camera shake.

Custom Modes (C1, C2, C3) – Save Your Favorite Settings

- The EOS R5 Mark II allows you to save custom settings to C1, C2, or C3 on the mode dial.
- For example, you can set C1 for portraits, C2 for landscapes, and C3 for video.
- This saves time when switching between different shooting scenarios.

Customize these modes in the Camera Menu > Custom Shooting Mode (C1-C3) > Register Settings.

Video Mode – Cinematic Recording at Your Fingertips

- Switch to Video Mode to record 8K or 4K video with professional-level settings.
- Adjust frame rates, recording formats, and focus settings for cinematic results.
- Use Log profiles (Canon Log 3) for better dynamic range in post-production.

If you're serious about video, explore custom video settings and external recording options.

Which Mode Should You Use?

Photography Type	Best Camera Mode
Portraits	Aperture Priority (Av)
Landscapes	Aperture Priority (Av)
Sports & Action	Shutter Priority (Tv)
Low Light & Night	Manual (M) or Bulb (B)
Street Photography	Program (P) or Aperture Priority (Av)
Everyday Snapshots	Auto or Scene Modes
Video Recording	Video Mode

Mastering Autofocus and Manual Focus

Focusing correctly is one of the most critical aspects of photography and videography. The Canon EOS R5 Mark II is equipped with Dual Pixel Autofocus II (DPAF II), an advanced autofocus (AF) system that provides fast, accurate, and intelligent subject tracking. However, there are situations where manual focus (MF) is the better choice for precision control.

In this section, we will explore the different autofocus modes, settings, techniques, and when to use manual focus to get sharp, professional-looking images.

Understanding Canon's Dual Pixel Autofocus II

The Canon EOS R5 Mark II uses Dual Pixel Autofocus II, which enhances speed, accuracy, and subject detection. This system provides:

■ Fast and accurate subject tracking – Detects and locks onto moving subjects quickly.

■ Eye, face, and body detection – Ideal for portraits and candid shots.

■ Animal and vehicle tracking – Recognizes pets, birds, and even race cars.

■ Full sensor coverage – Autofocus points cover nearly 100% of the sensor for flexibility.

■ Low-light focusing – Works efficiently even in dim lighting conditions. This makes autofocus highly reliable whether you're shooting stills or videos.

Autofocus (AF) Modes and When to Use Them

The Canon EOS R5 Mark II offers multiple AF modes for different scenarios.

❢ One-Shot AF

◆ Ideal for portraits, landscapes, or product photography.

◆ Locks focus on a subject and holds it until you take the photo.

◆ If the subject moves, you must ref

Mastering Autofocus and Manual Focus

🕯 AI Servo AF (Best for Moving Subjects)
◆ Perfect for sports, wildlife, and action photography.
◆ Continuously tracks and adjusts focus when the subject moves.
◆ Works with burst mode for capturing sharp sequences.
📌 Tip: Works well with high-speed continuous shooting (up to 30 fps) for action shots.

🕯 AI Focus AF (Hybrid Mode)
◆ Automatically switches between One-Shot AF and AI Servo AF.
◆ Starts as One-Shot AF, but if the subject moves, it shifts to AI Servo AF.
◆ Useful when photographing subjects that may suddenly start moving.
📌 Tip: Good for events, candid photography, and unpredictable movement.

Autofocus Area Modes

The EOS R5 Mark II allows you to choose where the Camera focuses using different area modes.

🔍 Spot AF (Pinpoint Focus)
• Focuses on a small, precise area for detail shots.
• Best for macro photography or product shots.

🔍 1-Point AF (Single Focus Point)
• Lets you manually select one focus point.
• Best for portraits, still life, and carefully composed shots.

🔍 Expand AF Area (More Flexibility)
• Uses one focus point but adds nearby points for better tracking.
• Best for wildlife or slightly moving subjects.

🔍 Zone AF (Larger Focus Area)
• Divides the frame into zones and focuses on the subject within that area.
• Best for group portraits or subjects moving in a predictable direction.

🔍 Whole Area AF (Automatic Selection)
- Uses intelligent subject tracking to find and follow subjects.
- Best for fast-moving subjects, action photography, and unpredictable movement.

📌 Tip: For more creative control, use 1-Point AF or Spot AF for precise focusing.

Face, Eye, and Subject Tracking AF

One of the biggest strengths of the EOS R5 Mark II is its advanced AI-powered subject tracking.

👀 Eye Detection AF
- ◆ Automatically locks focus on a subject's eye, ensuring sharp portraits.
- ◆ Works well for people, pets, and wildlife.
- ◆ Can detect both human and animal eyes.

🐎 Vehicle Tracking AF
- ◆ Recognizes and tracks cars, motorcycles, and race vehicles.
- ◆ Helps sports photographers capture fast-moving vehicles with precision.

📌 Tip: Enable Face + Eye Detection AF in the camera menu for better portrait photography.

Autofocus Tips for Stills and Video

📷 For photography:
- ■ Use One-Shot AF for portraits and still subjects.
- ■ Use AI Servo AF for sports, wildlife, or kids playing.
- ■ Select Zone AF for group portraits or moving subjects in a defined area.
- ■ Use Eye Detection AF for sharp eyes in portraits.

🎬 For Video:
- ■ Enable Movie Servo AF for continuous focus in videos.
- ■ Use Face + Eye Detection for vlogging or interviews.
- ■ Adjust AF speed and responsiveness for smooth focus transitions.

Mastering Autofocus and Manual Focus

■ Use Manual Focus Override if autofocus struggles in low light.

📌 Tip: If autofocus keeps shifting focus in videos, reduce the AF sensitivity in the menu.

When to Use Manual Focus (MF)

Autofocus is powerful, but sometimes manual focus is the best choice.

■ Low Light – Autofocus may struggle, so manual focus ensures accuracy.

■ Macro Photography – Precise focusing is needed for close-up shots.

■ Astrophotography – Helps focus on distant stars without hunting.

■ Videography – Allows smooth focus pulls without sudden AF shifts.

7. How to Use Manual Focus on the EOS R5 Mark II

🔧 Step 1: Switch to Manual Focus (MF)

1. Set the lens focus switch to MF.
2. In the Camera AF menu, choose Manual Focus.

🔧 Step 2: Use Focus Peaking

- Turn on Focus Peaking in the menu.
- The Camera will highlight the sharpest areas in red, yellow, or blue.
- Adjust focus until the important part of the image is highlighted.

🔧 Step 3: Use Magnification for Precision

- Press the Magnify button (+) to zoom in on the area you want to focus.
- Adjust the focus ring until the image appears sharp.

📌 Tip: Use Focus Guide (a digital focus assist tool) for even more accuracy.

Autofocus vs. Manual Focus: When to Use Each

Scenario	Best Focus Mode
Portraits	Eye Detection AF
Sports & Action	AI Servo AF
Wildlife	AI Servo AF + Tracking
Low Light	Manual Focus
Macro Photography	Manual focus + Focus Peaking
Videography	Manual focus for controlled focus shifts
Landscape	One-Shot AF + 1-Point AF

Image Quality and File Formats

The Canon EOS R5 Mark II is designed to deliver exceptional image quality, whether you're shooting stills or video. However, choosing the right file format and image settings is essential for getting the best results based on your needs.

In this chapter, we'll explore:

■ Different image formats (JPEG, RAW, HEIF, etc.)
■ How file formats affect quality and editing flexibility
■ Choosing the right settings for different scenarios

By the end of this chapter, you'll know how to optimize your image quality for every shoot.

Understanding Image Quality Settings

When you take a photo, the camera processes and saves the image in a specific format. The format you choose affects:

- Image quality (sharpness, colors, and detail).
- File size (storage space needed).
- Editing flexibility (how much you can adjust in post-processing).

The Canon EOS R5 Mark II offers several image file types, each with its advantages.

JPEG vs. RAW vs HEIF

File Format	Best For	Pros	Cons
JPEG	Everyday photography, social media, fast sharing	Small file size, ready-to-use, widely supported	Less editing flexibility, compression reduces quality
RAW	Professional photography, detailed editing	Maximum quality, high dynamic range, better for post-processing	Large file size, requires editing software
C-RAW (Compressed RAW)	Saving storage while keeping RAW benefits	Smaller than RAW, retains flexibility	Slightly less detail than full RAW
HEIF (High Efficiency Image Format)	Advanced shooters, HDR photography	Better quality than JPEG at smaller sizes, supports HDR	Not widely supported yet

Image Quality and File Formats

Tip: If you want the best balance of quality and file size, shoot in C-RAW.

JPEG: Quick and Convenient

JPEG is the most common image format. The Camera processes the image, applies sharpening, contrast, and color adjustments, then compresses the file to make it smaller.

JPEG Quality Settings:

- JPEG Fine: Best quality, but larger file size.
- JPEG Normal: Balanced size and quality.
- JPEG Basic: Smallest file size, lower quality.

📌 Best for:

✓ Everyday photography

✓ Social media and quick sharing

✓ When you don't plan to edit much

📌 Not ideal for:

✕ Professional editing (loss of details)

✕ Printing large images

RAW: Maximum Quality & Editing Flexibility

RAW files capture all the image data without compression, allowing for:

- Better color grading and adjustments.
- More control over exposure and shadows.
- Higher dynamic range, preserving details in bright and dark areas

Types of RAW Files in the EOS R5 Mark II:

⬛ RAW: Full-size, highest quality.

⬛ C-RAW (Compressed RAW): Smaller than RAW, but still high quality.

📌 Best for:

✓ Professional photography

✓ Editing in Lightroom, Photoshop, or Capture One

✓ Retaining maximum details

📌 Not ideal for:

✕ Direct sharing (must be converted first)

✕ Saving storage space

📌 Tip: Use C-RAW to save space while keeping RAW flexibility.

Image Quality and File Formats

HEIF: The Future of High-Quality Imaging

HEIF (High Efficiency Image Format) is a modern alternative to JPEG that provides:

■ Better quality than JPEG at the same or smaller file size.

■ 10-bit color depth, meaning more vibrant colors.

■ HDR compatibility, great for high dynamic range photography.

📌 Best for:

✓ Advanced photographers

✓ HDR photography

✓ Future-proofing files

📌 Not ideal for:

✗ Editing in all software (some programs don't support HEIF yet)

✗ Printing (JPEG or TIFF is preferred)

📌 Tip: If you're shooting HDR photos, HEIF is a great option.

Choosing the Best Image Size and Compression

To customize image quality, go to:

📌 Menu > Image Quality

There, you'll find different options:

- RAW + JPEG (saves both formats)
- JPEG Fine/Normal/Basic
- C-RAW vs. RAW

What Should You Choose?

✓ RAW or C-RAW for pro work.

✓ JPEG Fine for fast workflow.

✓ HEIF if you want high quality in small tiles.

📌 Tip: If you're unsure, shoot in RAW + JPEG to get the best of both worlds.

What About TIFF Files?

The Canon EOS R5 Mark II does not shoot directly in TIFF, but you can convert RAW files to TIFF in Canon's Digital Photo Professional (DPP) software.

TIFF is useful for:

- High-quality printing
- Archival storage

📌 Tip: Use RAW   TIFF conversion for professional prints.

Image Quality and File Formats

📌 Tip: Use RAW   TIFF conversion for professional prints.

Understanding Bit Depth and Color Depth

- JPEG = 8-bit (16 million colors)
- RAW = 12-bit or 14-bit (billions of colors)
- HEIF = 10-bit (more colors than JPEG, less than RAW)

📌 Tip: More bits = better colors and smoother gradations.

Video File Formats: Choosing the Right One

The Canon EOS R5 Mark II supports several video formats, including:

Format	Best For	Pros	Cons
MP4 (H.264)	General video, easy editing	Small file size, widely supported	Lower quality
MP4 (H.265/HEVC)	4K/8K video, high efficiency	Better compression, higher quality	Needs powerful computer to edit
RAW Video	Professional filmmaking	Maximum quality, great for grading	Huge file sizes

📌 Tip: If you plan to edit heavily, shoot in RAW video or H.265.

How to Choose the Right File Format for You

Shooting	Recommended Format
Everyday photos	JPEG Fine
Professional work	RAW or C-RAW
Editing flexibility	RAW
HDR photography	HEIF
Fast workflow	RAW

Image Quality and File Formats

Video for social media	MP4 (H.264)
High-end video production	RAW Video

📌 Tip: If you plan to edit heavily, shoot in RAW video or H.265. How to Choose the Right File Format for You

Advance Camera Setting

The Canon EOS R5 Mark II is packed with advanced settings that allow you to fine-tune your Camera for maximum performance and creative control. Understanding these settings will help you capture sharper images, better colors, and more dynamic shots in different conditions.
In this chapter, we'll explore:

■ White balance for accurate colors
■ ISO and noise control
■ Picture Styles and custom settings
■ HDR, bracketing, and dynamic range features
■ Highlight Tone Priority and Auto Lighting Optimizer

By mastering these settings, you can customize your Camera for any shooting scenario.

White Balance (WB) – Getting Accurate Colors

White balance (WB) controls how the Camera interprets colors under different lighting conditions. If set incorrectly, your images may look too warm (yellowish) or too cool (bluish).

White Balance Presets in EOS R5 Mark II

WB MODE	BEST FOR	COLOR EFFECT
Auto (AWB)	General use	Adjusts automatically
Daylight	Sunny outdoor shots	Warmer tones
Shade	Cloudy or shaded areas	Warmer colors
Cloudy	Overcast days	Adds warmth
Tungsten	Indoor shots with yellow lighting	Reduces warm tones
Fluorescent	Office or white LED lighting	Reduces green tint

Advance Camera Setting

Flash	Flash photography	Adjusts for flash color
Custom WB	Critical color accuracy	Uses a reference photo

📌 Tip: If your photos look too yellow or blue, adjust the White Balance (WB) manually.

. ISO Sensitivity – Balancing Light and Noise

ISO controls the Camera's sensitivity to light. A low ISO (100-400) keeps images sharp, while a high ISO (3200-51200) lets you shoot in low light but adds noise (graininess).

Recommended ISO Settings

■ ISO 100-400 – Best for daylight and bright conditions (low noise).

■ ISO 800-1600 – Good for indoor photography with some light.

■ ISO 3200-6400 – Use in low light (concerts, night shots, indoor events).

■ ISO 12800+ – Emergency setting for dark environments (visible noise).

📌 Tip: Use Auto ISO for quick adjustments, but set a maximum limit (e.g., 6400) to avoid excessive noise.

Picture Styles – Controlling the Look of Your Photos

Picture Styles affect how the Camera processes colors, contrast, and sharpness in JPEG and HEIF images.

Available Picture Styles in EOS R5 Mark II

Advance Camera Setting

Style	Best For	Effect
Standard	General shooting	Balanced contrast and color
Portrait	Portrait photography	Softer skin tones, natural colors
Landscape	Scenery, nature shots	Boosted greens and blues
Neutral	Editing in post	Low contrast, natural tones
Faithful	Studio or product photography	Color accuracy in daylight
Monochrome	Black & white photos	Converts to grayscale
User Defined	Custom styles	Fully customizable settings

📌 Tip: Use Neutral or Faithful if you plan to edit your images later.

Dynamic Range and HDR Features
HDR Mode – High Dynamic Range Photography
HDR mode captures multiple exposures and blends them for better shadow and highlight details.

Advance Camera Setting

How to Enable HDR Mode:
1. Go to Menu > HDR Mode
2. Select Enable HDR Shooting
3. Choose Auto Align (ON) for handheld shots
4. Capture an image – the Camera blends exposures automatically

📌 Best for:

⬛ Landscapes – Preserves bright skies and dark foregrounds

⬛ Architectural photography – Keeps details in highlights and shadows

Exposure Bracketing – Capturing Multiple Exposures
Bracketing lets you capture multiple images at different exposure levels (one underexposed, one normal, one overexposed).

📌 How to Enable Bracketing:
1. Go to Menu > Exposure Compensation/AEB
2. Set the bracketing range (e.g., ±1, ±2 stops)
3. Press the shutter once, and the Camera takes multiple shots

📌 Best for:

⬛ HDR editing in post-processing

⬛ Scenes with extreme contrast (sunsets, bright windows)

Highlight Tone Priority – Preserving Highlights
Highlight Tone Priority (HTP) helps protect bright areas from overexposing. It's useful for shooting:

⬛ Bright landscapes (beaches, snow, sunlit scenes)

⬛ Weddings (white dresses, bright backgrounds)

📌 How to Enable HTP:

- Go to Menu > Highlight Tone Priority > Enable

  Note: Enabling HTP locks ISO to 200 or higher to preserve highlights.

Auto Lighting Optimizer (ALO) – Balancing exposure
Auto Lighting Optimizer (ALO) automatically adjusts shadow brightness without losing detail in highlights.

📌 Best for:

⬛ Shooting in harsh lighting

⬛ Keeping details in shadows and highlights

Advance Camera Setting

📌 How to Enable ALO:
1. Go to Menu > Auto Lighting Optimizer
2. Select Low / Standard / High

📌 Tip: If you shoot RAW, you can adjust shadows later instead of using ALO.

Customizing Your Camera for Faster Shooting

Assigning Custom Buttons

You can assign frequently used functions to specific buttons for faster access.

📌 How to Customize Buttons:
1. Go to Menu > Customize Buttons
2. Select a button (e.g., AF-ON, M-Fn)
3. Assign a function (ISO, White Balance, Eye AF, etc.)

📌 Tip: Assign Eye Detection AF to a button for quick access during portraits.

Using Custom Shooting Modes (C1, C2, C3)

Save frequently used settings to custom modes (C1, C2, C3) on the mode dial.

📌 How to Set Custom Modes:
1. Set your preferred settings (shutter speed, aperture, ISO, AF mode, etc.)
2. Go to Menu > Custom Shooting Mode (C1-C3)
3. Select Register Settings

📌 Tip: Set C1 for portraits, C2 for landscapes, and C3 for video settings.

Shooting Scenario	Recommended Settings
Portraits	WB: Daylight / ISO: 100-400 / Picture Style: Portrait
Landscapes	WB: Cloudy / ISO: 100 / Picture Style: Landscape
Low Light	WB: Auto / ISO: 1600+ / Noise Reduction: High

Advance Camera Setting

Sports & Action	WB: Auto / ISO: Auto (Max 6400) / AI Servo AF
Street Photography	WB: Auto / ISO: Auto (Max 3200) / Picture Style: Standard

📌 Tip: Adjust settings based on lighting conditions and personal style.

Exposure and Meeting

Exposure is the foundation of photography. It determines how bright or dark an image appears based on how much light reaches the camera sensor. To master the Canon EOS R5 Mark II, you need to understand exposure settings and how to use metering modes to get the best results in different lighting conditions.

In this chapter, we'll cover:

- ■ The Exposure Triangle (Shutter Speed, Aperture, ISO)
- ■ Understanding Metering Modes
- ■ Using Exposure Compensation
- ■ Best settings for different lighting conditions

The Exposure Triangle – Balancing Light and Motion

The three main factors that control exposure are:

- Shutter Speed (Controls Motion Blur)
- Aperture (Controls Depth of Field)
- ISO (Controls Brightness & Noise)

When you adjust one setting, you may need to compensate with another to maintain proper exposure.

Setting	What It Controls	Effect on Image
Shutter Speed	Controls motion	Faster = Freezes motion / Slower = Motion blur
Aperture (f-number)	Controls background blur (depth of field)	Lower f-number = Blurry background / Higher f-number = Sharp background
ISO	Controls brightness	Lower ISO = Cleaner image / Higher ISO = More noise

✦ Tip: Use the Camera's Exposure Meter in the viewfinder or LCD screen to see if your shot is properly exposed.

Exposure and Meeting

Understanding Shutter Speed (How Fast the Camera Captures Light)

Shutter speed is measured in fractions of a second (e.g., 1/1000s, 1/250s, 1/30s).

Shutter Speed	Best For	Effect
1/2000s - 1/1000s	Fast-moving subjects (sports, wildlife)	Freezes action
1/500s - 1/250s	General photography	Eliminates minor motion blur
1/125s - 1/60s	Portraits, street photography	Balanced motion
1/30s - 1s	Low-light photography	Can introduce motion blur
Long exposure (1s - 30s)	Night photography, light trails	Captures motion over time

Understanding Aperture (How Much Light Enters the Lens)

Aperture is measured in f-stops (f/1.8, f/4, f/11, etc.).

- Lower f-numbers (f/1.2 – f/2.8): More light, blurred background (good for portraits).
- Higher f-numbers (f/8 – f/16): Less light, everything in focus (good for landscapes).

Aperture (f-stop)	Best For	Effect
f/1.2 - f/2.8	Portraits, low light	Blurred background (shallow depth of field)
f/4 - f/8	Street, travel photography	Moderate background blur
f/11 - f/16	Landscapes, group photos	Everything in focus (deep depth of field)

Exposure and Meeting

Understanding ISO (Light Sensitivity and Noise Control)

ISO adjusts the Camera's sensitivity to light.

- Low ISO (100-400): Clean, noise-free images.
- High ISO (3200+): Brighter images but more grain (noise).

ISO Level	Best For	Effect
100-400	Daylight, bright conditions	Cleanest image
800-1600	Indoors, cloudy days	Minimal noise
3200-6400	Low light, concerts	Some noise but usable
12800+	Extreme low light	High noise, loss of detail

📌 Tip: Use Auto ISO with a max limit (e.g., 6400) to prevent excessive noise.

Metering Modes – How the Camera Reads Light

The Canon EOS R5 Mark II has several metering modes to determine exposure.

❢ Evaluative Metering (Best for Most Situations)
✓ Measures light across the entire frame
✓ Best for general photography
❢ Spot Metering (Best for High Contrast Scenes)
✓ Measures only 2-3% of the frame
✓ Best for portraits, bright backgrounds, and backlit subjects
❢ Partial Metering (Larger Spot Metering)
✓ Measures about 10% of the frame
✓ Best for portraits and subjects with strong backlight
❢ Center-Weighted Average Metering
✓ Prioritizes the center of the frame
✓ Best for balanced lighting situations
📌 Tip: Use Spot Metering for portraits against bright backgrounds (like sunsets) to avoid underexposing the subject.

Exposure and Meeting

Using Exposure Compensation (+/- Button)

Exposure Compensation allows you to adjust brightness without changing shutter speed, aperture, or ISO.

📌 How to Adjust Exposure Compensation:

1. Turn the Main Dial (near the shutter button) to increase (+) or decrease (-) exposure.
2. +1 or +2: Brightens the image (use in dark scenes).
3. -1 or -2: Darkens the image (use in bright conditions).

📌 Tip: If a scene looks too dark or too bright, adjust Exposure Compensation instead of manually changing settings.

Best Exposure and Metering Settings for Different Conditions

Shooting Scenario	Recommended Settings
Portraits	Aperture: f/2.8 - f/5.6 / Spot Metering
Landscapes	Aperture: f/8 - f/16 / Evaluative Metering
Sports & Action	Shutter Speed: 1/1000s+ / AI Servo AF / Evaluative Metering
Low Light & Night	ISO: 3200+ / Shutter Speed: 1/30s+ / Spot Metering
Backlit Subjects	Spot Metering / Exposure Compensation (+1 or +2)

📌 Tip: Always review your histogram to check exposure accuracy.

8. Using the Histogram for Perfect Exposure

The Histogram is a graph that shows how light is distributed in your image.

- Left Side = Shadows (Black areas)
- Middle = Midtones (Balanced exposure)
- Right Side = Highlights (Bright areas)

Exposure and Meeting

How to Read the Histogram:
- ■ A balanced curve means a well-exposed image.
- ■ A graph leaning left means the image is too dark (underexposed).
- ■ A graph leaning right means the image is too bright (overexposed).
- 📌 Tip: Enable Highlight Alerts in the camera menu to see overexposed areas flashing in the image review.

Mastering exposure and metering allows you to capture perfectly lit images in any condition. By understanding:
- ■ The Exposure Triangle (Shutter Speed, Aperture, ISO)
- ■ Metering Modes for different lighting
- ■ Using Exposure Compensation
- ■ Reading the Histogram for better control

You'll be able to take control of your Canon EOS R5 Mark II and create stunning images every time.

Next, we'll dive into Chapter 7: Mastering Video Recording, where we explore 8K & 4K video settings, cinematic techniques, and stabilization features.

Mastering Video Recording

The Canon EOS R5 Mark II is a powerful video camera, capable of shooting 8K RAW, 4K HQ, and high-frame-rate slow motion. Whether you're creating cinematic films, vlogs, documentaries, or professional content, understanding its video features will help you get the best results.

In this chapter, we'll cover:

■ Video resolutions, frame rates, and file formats
■ Best settings for cinematic video
■ Autofocus and stabilization for smooth footage
■ Audio recording tips and external mic options
■ Best practices for professional-looking videos

By the end, you'll know how to optimize your Canon EOS R5 Mark II for high-quality video production.

1. Video Resolutions and Frame Rates – Choosing the Right Quality

The EOS R5 Mark II supports multiple resolutions and frame rates, allowing for high-resolution cinematic footage or slow-motion effects.

Resolution	Frame Rates	Best For
8K (8192 x 4320)	30p, 24p	Maximum detail, professional filmmaking
4K HQ (High Quality)	60p, 30p, 24p	Downsampled from 8K for sharp 4K video
4K Standard	120p, 60p, 30p, 24p	High-speed action, cinematic quality
Full HD (1080p)	180p, 120p, 60p, 30p, 24p	Slow motion, social media content

Choosing the Right Video Format (Codec and Bitrate)

The EOS R5 Mark II records in multiple formats, including MP4, All-I, and RAW video.

Mastering Video Recording

Format	Best For	File Size	Post-Processing
MP4 (H.264)	General use, web videos	Small	Easy to edit
MP4 (H.265 HEVC)	High efficiency, 4K HDR	Medium	Requires powerful computer
All-I (Intra-Frame)	Professional editing	Large	High-quality, smooth playback
8K/4K RAW	High-end filmmaking	Very large	Maximum flexibility

📌 Tip: Use H.265 for high-quality, small file sizes and RAW for serious film work.

Best Camera Settings for Cinematic Video
For professional-looking videos, use these settings:
📌 Frame Rate:
- 24p – Classic cinematic look
- 30p – Smooth and natural motion
- 60p+ – High-speed motion or slow-motion effects

📌 Shutter Speed Rule:
🎬 Shutter speed = 2x frame rate (for natural motion blur)
- 24p   1/50s
- 30p   1/60s
- 60p   1/125s

📌 aperture:
- Use f/2.8 or lower for soft backgrounds (shallow depth of field).
- Use f/8 - f/11 for landscapes and wide shots.

📌 ISO:
- Keep it at 100-800 for clean footage.
- Use higher ISOs only if necessary.

Mastering Video Recording

📌 Picture Profile:
- Canon Log 3 (C-Log3) – Best for color grading in post.
- Neutral – For straight-out-of-camera use.
- HDR PQ – For high dynamic range videos.

📌 Tip: If you plan to edit heavily, shoot in C-Log 3 for better dynamic range.

Mastering Autofocus for Video

The Canon EOS R5 Mark II has an intelligent Dual Pixel Autofocus (DPAF II) system, perfect for smooth, cinematic focusing.
Best Autofocus Settings for Video:

⬛ Face + Eye Detection AF – Best for interviews and vlogging.
⬛ Subject Tracking AF – Follows people, pets, and vehicles.
⬛ Touch Focus – Tap the screen to focus on different areas.
⬛ Manual Focus with Focus Peaking – Best for cinematic focus pulls.

📌 Tip: Reduce AF Speed & Sensitivity (Menu > AF settings) for smooth focus transitions.

Using Image Stabilization for Smooth Footage

The EOS R5 Mark II has In-Body Image Stabilization (IBIS) + Digital IS, which helps reduce shake.

Stabilization Mode	Best For	Effect
IBIS (Sensor Shift)	Handhold shooting	Reduces small shakes
Digital IS	Walking shots	Additional stabilization
Gimbal + IBIS	Cinematic shots	Super steady footage

📌 Tip: Use a gimbal for ultra-smooth movement shots.

Mastering Video Recording

Recording High-Quality Audio
Good audio is just as important as video quality.
Built-in vs. External Microphones:

Mic Type	Best For
Built-in Mic	Casual videos, home use
Shotgun Mic (Rode VideoMic Pro)	Interviews, vlogging
Lavalier Mic (Wireless)	Presentations, talking on Camera
External Recorder (Zoom H5, Tascam DR-40X)	Professional audio

📌 Tip: Use an external mic for the best sound quality.

Controlling Exposure with ND Filters
In bright conditions, you need ND (Neutral Density) filters to control light without changing settings.
- ND4 (2 stops) – Slightly reduces brightness.
- ND8 (3 stops) – Perfect for daytime video.
- ND16+ (4+ stops) – Use in bright sunlight.

📌 Tip: ND filters allow you to keep shutter speed low while filming in bright conditions.

Heat Management & Avoiding Overheating
Recording 8K or 4K at high frame rates can cause overheating.
📌 How to Prevent Overheating:
- Use an external recorder to offload processing.
- Record in 4K HQ instead of 8K when possible.
- Turn off the LCD screen when not needed.
- Use a cooling fan or external heat sink for long shoots.

Mastering Video Recording

Best Video Settings for Different Shooting Scenarios

Scenario	Resolution / Frame Rate	Best Settings
Cinematic Film	4K HQ, 24p	C-Log 3, ND filter, IBIS
YouTube / Vlogs	4K, 30p	Face AF, external mic
Slow Motion	4K 120p	High shutter speed, manual focus
Interviews	4K, 24p	Face AF, shotgun mic
Low Light	4K, 24p	ISO 800-3200, wide aperture
Action Sports	4K 120p	Fast shutter, AI Servo AF

📌 Tip: Use manual focus for slow-motion shots to prevent focus hunting.

Editing and Exporting Video

Once you've recorded your footage, editing is the final step.

Best Video Editing Software:

◼ Adobe Premiere Pro – Industry standard for filmmakers.

◼ DaVinci Resolve – Best for color grading.

◼ Final Cut Pro – Fast editing for Mac users.

📌 Export Settings for YouTube & Social Media:

- Resolution: 4K (3840 x 2160)
- Format: MP4 (H.264 or H.265)
- Bitrate: 50 Mbps (4K), 20 Mbps (1080p)
- Audio: AAC 320kbps

📌 Tip: Always export in high quality to avoid compression loss on YouTube.

Final Thoughts

Mastering video recording on the Canon EOS R5 Mark II means understanding:

■ The best resolutions & frame rates
■ Autofocus and stabilization techniques
■ How to record professional audio
■ Avoiding overheating for long shoots
■ Using ND filters to control exposure

Now that you know how to shoot professional video, in the next chapter, we'll explore Creative Features and Special Modes, including time-lapse, multiple exposure, and focus stacking.

Creative Features and Special Modes

Time-Lapse and Interval Timer Shooting
■ What is Time-Lapse?
Time-lapse photography stitches together a sequence of photos taken over time to create a fast-motion video. This is great for:
■ Cloud movements and sunsets
■ Cityscapes and traffic trails
■ Stars and night sky motion
📌 How to Set Up Time-Lapse on the EOS R5 Mark II:
■ Go to Menu > Time-Lapse Movie
■ Select Enable
■ Choose your Interval (Time Between Shots)
- Example: 5 sec for slow-moving clouds, 30 sec for sunset
- ■ Choose your Total Number of Shots
- ■ Set Resolution (4K or 8K)
- ■ Start recording

📌 Tip: Use a tripod to avoid camera movement and keep the video smooth.

Multiple Exposure Mode – Artistic Image Blending
■ What is Multiple Exposure?
This feature allows you to combine multiple images into a single frame, creating surreal, artistic effects without post-processing.
📌 How to Enable Multiple Exposure Mode:
■ Go to Menu > Multiple Exposure
■ Select Enable
■ Choose Number of Exposures (2-9 images)
■ Set Overlay Mode:
- Additive: Merges images with equal brightness
- Average: Balances exposure
- Bright/Dark: Prioritizes bright or dark areas
- ■ Take the first image, then align the second for creative effects

📌 Best Uses for Multiple Exposure:
■ Double exposure portraits (blending a person with textures like trees or water)
■ Layering movement (like a dancer's motion)
■ Creative storytelling

Creative Features and Special Modes

Focus Stacking and Focus Bracketing – Ultimate Sharpness

■ What is Focus Stacking?

Focus stacking lets you combine multiple images with different focus points to create one ultra-sharp image. It's commonly used in macro photography, landscapes, and product photography.

📌 How to Enable Focus Bracketing (for Stacking Later):

■ Go to Menu > Focus Bracketing

■ Set Enable

■ Choose Number of Shots (3-99)

■ Adjust Focus Step Size (Small for macro, Medium for general shots)

■ Press the shutter once—the Camera will take multiple shots with different focus points

📌 Tip: You will need software like Photoshop or Helicon Focus to stack the images together.

■ Best for:

- Macro shots (flowers, insects, small objects)
- Product photography (sharpness from front to back)
- Landscapes (sharp details in foreground & background)

Dual Pixel RAW – Micro-Adjustments After Shooting

■ What is Dual Pixel RAW?

Dual Pixel RAW allows you to fine-tune focus, adjust bokeh, and reduce ghosting AFTER taking the photo.

📌 How to Enable Dual Pixel RAW:

■ Go to Menu > Image Quality

■ Select Dual Pixel RAW: Enable

■ Shoot in RAW Mode

■ Open the file in Canon's Digital Photo Professional (DPP) software

■ Adjust:

- Micro Focus Shift – Adjust focus slightly forward or backward
- Bokeh Shift – Change background blur slightly
- Ghosting Reduction – Reduce light flare

📌 Tip: Use this feature only in well-lit, controlled conditions to get the best results.

■ Best for:

- Portraits (fine-tuning sharpness on the eyes)

- Correcting slight focus errors
- Enhancing bokeh placement

Custom Shooting Modes (C1, C2, C3) – Quick Access to Favorite Settings

If you often switch between different shooting styles (e.g., portraits, landscapes, video), you can save your preferred settings to C1, C2, and C3 on the mode dial for quick access.

📌 How to Save Custom Shooting Modes:

◼ Set up your Camera with your preferred settings (aperture, shutter speed, ISO, focus mode, etc.).

◼ Go to Menu > Custom Shooting Mode (C1-C3) > Register Settings.

◼ Assign to C1, C2, or C3.

◼ Now, simply turn the mode dial to C1, C2, or C3 for quick access!

◼ Best Uses for Custom Modes:

- C1: Portraits (Aperture Priority, Eye AF, Soft Colors)
- C2: Landscapes (Manual Mode, f/11, Low ISO)
- C3: Video (4K, 24fps, Face Tracking AF)

📌 Tip: This saves time and ensures consistency in different shooting scenarios.

Silent Shutter Mode – Stealthy Shooting

The Canon EOS R5 Mark II has a silent electronic shutter, perfect for:

◼ Weddings and events (no distracting shutter sound)

◼ Wildlife photography (no noise to scare animals)

◼ Concerts and theaters (silent shooting in low light)

📌 How to Enable Silent Shutter Mode:

◼ Go to Menu > Shutter Mode

◼ Select Electronic (Silent)

📌 Tip: Silent mode is great for stealth photography, but may introduce rolling shutter issues with fast-moving subjects.

Anti-Flicker Shooting – Better Results Under Artificial Lights

Fluorescent and LED lights can cause flickering in images. The Anti-Flicker Mode helps by adjusting shutter timing to match the light's cycle.

Creative Features and Special Modes

- 📌 How to Enable Anti-Flicker Mode:
- ■ Go to Menu > Anti-Flicker Shooting
- ■ Select Enable
- ■ Best for:
- Indoor sports photography
- Event photography under artificial lighting

Best Settings for Different Creative Modes

Creative Mode	Best Settings	Best Used For
Time-Lapse	Interval: 5-30 sec, Tripod	Sunsets, traffic, night sky
Multiple Exposure	Additive mode, 2-3 shots	Artistic portraits, surreal effects
Focus Stacking	10-30 shots, Small focus steps	Macro, product shots
Dual Pixel RAW	RAW + Dual Pixel enabled	Portrait retouching, micro-focus tweaks
Silent Shutter	Electronic mode	Weddings, wildlife
Custom Modes (C1-C3)	Pre-save favorite settings	Quick shooting setup

The Canon EOS R5 Mark II isn't just about high-resolution images—it's also a powerful creative tool. By using:

■ Time-lapse for motion storytelling
■ Multiple exposure for artistic effects
■ focus stacking for ultimate sharpness
■ Dual Pixel RAW for fine adjustments
■ Custom shooting modes for efficiency

You can take your photography to the next level and capture images that stand out.In the next chapter, we'll explore Wireless Connectivity and Remote Control, where you'll learn how to transfer images, use the Canon Camera Connect app, and shoot remotely.

Wireless Connectivity and Remote Control

The Canon EOS R5 Mark II is equipped with advanced wireless features, allowing you to transfer images, control the Camera remotely, and connect to other devices without cables. Whether you need to send files to your smartphone, control the Camera from a distance, or back up your images wirelessly, this chapter will walk you through all the options.

In this session , we'll cover:

■ Wi-Fi and Bluetooth setup

■ Transferring photos and videos to smartphones & computers

■ Using the Canon Camera Connect app

■ Remote shooting options (smartphone, remote shutter, tethering)

■ Wireless printing and cloud storage

By the end of this chapter, you'll be able to seamlessly connect and control your Camera without limitations.

Setting Up Wi-Fi and Bluetooth on the Canon EOS R5 Mark II

To use wireless features, you need to first enable Wi-Fi and Bluetooth on the Camera.

🎥 How to Enable Wi-Fi & Bluetooth:

■ Go to Menu > Wireless Communication Settings

■ Select Wi-Fi Settings > Enable

■ Select Bluetooth Settings > Enable

■ The Camera will now be ready to pair with a smartphone, tablet, or computer

🎥 Tip: Bluetooth allows for automatic reconnection, while Wi-Fi enables fast file transfers.

Transferring Photos and Videos to a Smartphone

Using the Canon Camera Connect app, you can wirelessly transfer photos and videos to your iPhone or Android device.

🎥 How to Transfer Files to a Smartphone:

■ Install the Canon Camera Connect App from the App Store or Google Play

■ Open the app and pair the Camera via Wi-Fi or Bluetooth

■ Select Images on Camera to browse and download files

■ Choose your preferred photos and transfer them to your phone

■ Best for:
- Quickly sharing photos on social media
- Backing up images to your cloud storage
- Editing pictures on a mobile app like Lightroom Mobile

📌 Tip: Use Wi-Fi Direct for faster transfers instead of Bluetooth.

Transferring Photos to a Computer (PC/Mac)

You can also transfer files directly to your computer without needing cables.

📌 How to Transfer Files to a Computer Wirelessly:

■ Install Canon EOS Utility on your PC/Mac

■ Enable Wi-Fi on the Camera (Menu > Wireless Settings > Enable Wi-Fi)

■ Connect to the same Wi-Fi network as your computer

■ Open EOS Utility and select Remote File Transfer

■ Browse and download your images directly to your computer storage

■ Best for:
- Quickly backing up RAW files
- Wireless tethering to a computer
- Working in a studio setup without cables

📌 Tip: Use 5GHz Wi-Fi for faster transfer speeds than 2.4GHz.

Using Canon Camera Connect for Remote Shooting

One of the best features of Canon Camera Connect is remote shooting, which allows you to control your Camera from your phone.

📌 How to Enable Remote Shooting:

■ Open the Canon Camera Connect App

■ Connect to the Camera via Wi-Fi

■ Select Remote Live View Shooting

■ Adjust shutter speed, aperture, ISO, and focus from the app

■ Tap the shutter button on your phone to capture photos remotely

■ Best for:
- Self-portraits and group shots without a timer
- Wildlife photography (avoiding camera shake)
- Long-exposure shots (remotely trigger without touching the Camera)

📌 Tip: Use a tripod for stable remote shooting.

Wireless Connectivity and Remote Control

Remote Control with Canon's BR-E1 Wireless Shutter

If you need a physical remote control, Canon offers the BR-E1 Bluetooth Remote for wirelessly triggering the shutter.

📌 How to Pair Canon BR-E1 Remote:

◼ Go to Menu > Wireless Communication Settings

◼ Select Bluetooth Function > Remote Control

◼ Hold the pairing button on the BR-E1 until the Camera recognizes it

◼ Once paired, press the remote shutter button to capture images

◼ Best for:

- Landscape photography (avoiding camera shake)
- Astrophotography and long-exposure shots
- Self-portraits and tripod setups

📌 Tip: The BR-E1 does NOT require line of sight, unlike IR remotes.

Tethered Shooting for Professional Workflows

📌 What is Tethered Shooting?

Tethering allows you to connect your Camera to a computer and view images live on a large screen as you shoot.

◼ Best for:

- Studio photography (portraits, products)
- Fashion shoots where instant previews are needed
- Commercial photography for precise adjustments

How to Set Up Tethered Shooting (Wired or Wireless):

📌 Wired (USB-C Connection to Lightroom or Capture One)

◼ Connect the Camera to a computer via USB-C

◼ Open Lightroom, Capture One, or EOS Utility

◼ Enable Tethered Shooting Mode

◼ Photos will appear directly on the computer as you shoot

📌 Wireless (Wi-Fi Tethering to EOS Utility):

◼ Enable Wi-Fi on the Camera

◼ Open Canon EOS Utility on your PC/Mac

◼ Select Remote Shooting Mode

◼ Capture and view images wirelessly on a big screen

📌 Tip: Use a fast memory card to prevent lag during tethering.

Wireless Connectivity and Remote Control

Wireless Printing – Print Directly from Your Camera

With Wi-Fi Direct, you can send images straight to a wireless printer without needing a computer.

📌 How to Print Wirelessly:

■ Go to Menu > Wireless Printing

■ Select Wi-Fi Printer

■ Choose the image to print and send it to the printer

■ Best for:

- Instant printing of travel or event photos
- On-the-go professional proofs

📌 Tip: Use Canon SELPHY Wireless Printers for fast, high-quality prints.

Cloud Backup and Online Storage Options

The EOS R5 Mark II can automatically upload images to the cloud for safe storage and easy access.

📌 How to Enable Canon Cloud Backup:

■ Go to Menu > Cloud Service

■ Sign in with your Canon ID

■ Select a cloud service (Google Drive, image.canon, etc.)

■ Enable Auto Upload for instant backups

■ Best for:

- Automatically backing up images after a shoot
- Accessing photos from any device (phone, tablet, laptop)
- Sharing high-quality images quickly

📌 Tip: Google Photos and Adobe Creative Cloud offer great cloud storage options.

Best Practices for Wireless Connectivity

Feature	Best Use Case	Tips
Wi-Fi Transfer to Phone	Social media, quick backups	Use 5GHz Wi-Fi for speed
Wi-Fi Transfer to PC	Studio and event photography	Keep Camera near router

Wireless Connectivity and Remote Control

Remote Shooting via App	Self-portraits, wildlife	Use tripod for stability
Tethered Shooting (USB/Wi-Fi)	Professional studio work	Use high-speed memory cards
Cloud Backup	Automatic storage	Ensure strong Wi-Fi connection

The Canon EOS R5 Mark II offers powerful wireless connectivity and remote control options, making it easier than ever to transfer, share, and control your Camera from anywhere. By using:

- Wi-Fi & Bluetooth for seamless transfers
- Remote shooting for hands-free photography
- Wireless tethering for professional workflows
- Cloud backup for instant photo storage

You can streamline your photography workflow and focus more on creativity.

Accessories and Lens Recommendations

The Canon EOS R5 Mark II is a professional-grade camera that delivers outstanding image and video quality, but to get the most out of it, you'll need the right accessories and lenses. Choosing the right gear can enhance performance, improve workflow, and protect your investment.
In this chapter, we'll cover:

■ Best lenses for different types of photography
■ Essential accessories (batteries, memory cards, tripods, etc.)
■ Audio equipment for high-quality video recording
■ External monitors and storage solutions
■ Protective gear and cleaning kits

By the end, you'll know exactly what you need to maximize the potential of your Canon EOS R5 Mark II.

Best Lenses for the Canon EOS R5 Mark II

The EOS R5 Mark II uses RF-mount lenses, but it also supports EF-mount lenses with an adapter. Here's a list of top lenses based on different photography styles.

■ Best Lenses for Portrait Photography
■ Canon RF 85mm f/1.2L USM – Ultimate sharpness, creamy bokeh
■ Canon RF 50mm f/1.2L USM – Classic portrait lens, beautiful background blur
■ Canon RF 70-200mm f/2.8L IS USM – Great for professional portraits and compression

📌 Tip: A wide aperture (f/1.2 – f/2.8) helps create soft, blurry backgrounds (bokeh).

■ Best Lenses for Landscape Photography
■ Canon RF 15-35mm f/2.8L IS USM – Ultra-wide, sharp from edge to edge
■ Canon RF 24-70mm f/2.8L IS USM – Versatile for landscapes and travel
■ Canon RF 14-35mm f/4L IS USM – Lighter, excellent for scenic views
📌 Tip: Use f/8 – f/16 for sharpness in landscapes.

Accessories and Lens Recommendations

🏃 Best Lenses for Sports & Wildlife Photography
⬛ Canon RF 100-500mm f/4.5-7.1L IS USM – Long reach, lightweight for handheld shooting
⬛ Canon RF 400mm f/2.8L IS USM – Professional sports and wildlife lens
⬛ Canon RF 600mm f/4L IS USM – Extreme reach for birds and distant subjects
📌 Tip: Use fast shutter speeds (1/1000s or faster) to freeze motion.

🔍 Best Lenses for Macro Photography
⬛ Canon RF 100mm f/2.8L Macro IS USM – 1.4x magnification, excellent stabilization
⬛ Canon RF 35mm f/1.8 IS Macro STM – Budget-friendly, great for close-ups
📌 Tip: Use Focus Bracketing for ultra-sharp macro images.

🎥 Best Lenses for Video & Vlogging
⬛ Canon RF 24-105mm f/4L IS USM – Versatile for handheld video
⬛ Canon RF 16mm f/2.8 STM – Compact, wide-angle for vlogging
⬛ Canon RF 28-70mm f/2L USM – Cinematic quality, sharp at all focal lengths
📌 Tip: Use a gimbal for smoother handheld shots.

Essential Accessories for the EOS R5 Mark II
🔋 Extra Batteries & Power Accessories
The EOS R5 Mark II uses the LP-E6NH battery, but video recording and continuous shooting drain power quickly.
⬛ Canon LP-E6NH Battery Pack – Official battery with maximum compatibility
⬛ Canon BG-R10 Battery Grip – Doubles battery life, adds vertical controls
⬛ Anker PowerCore+ 26800mAh – USB-C power bank for extended shoots
📌 Tip: Always carry at least two spare batteries for long shooting days.

Accessories and Lens Recommendations

■ High-Speed Memory Cards
The EOS R5 Mark II has dual card slots:
- Slot 1: CFexpress Type B
- Slot 2: SD UHS-II

■ SanDisk Extreme PRO CFexpress Type B (512GB) – Best for 8K RAW video

■ Lexar Professional 2000x UHS-II SD Card (128GB) – Fast SD card for 4K video & burst mode

📌 Tip: CFexpress cards are required for 8K and 4K high-frame-rate videos.

🎥 Tripods & Gimbals for Stable Shots
■ Manfrotto Befree Advanced Tripod – Lightweight travel tripod
■ Gitzo GT3543LS Systematic Tripod – Heavy-duty for landscapes and wildlife
■ DJI RS 3 Gimbal – For cinematic smooth video shots

📌 Tip: Use a tripod for landscapes & long exposures, and a gimbal for moving shots.

🎤 Audio Equipment for High-Quality Video
The EOS R5 Mark II has a built-in microphone, but for professional-quality sound, use an external mic.
■ RØDE VideoMic Pro+ – Best shotgun mic for vlogging and filmmaking
■ Sennheiser MKE 600 – Pro-level directional microphone
■ RØDE Wireless GO II – Compact wireless mic for interviews and vlogs

📌 Tip: Use an external audio recorder (Zoom H5, Tascam DR-40X) for higher-quality sound.

📺 External Monitors for Better Composition
■ Atomos Ninja V – 5-inch external monitor, great for video recording
■ SmallHD Focus 7 – 7-inch ultra-bright screen for professional shoots

📌 Tip: External monitors help when filming in bright sunlight or for accurate color grading.

Accessories and Lens Recommendations

■ External SSDs & Backup Storage
8K and 4K video files take up a lot of space, so a fast SSD is necessary.
■ Samsung T7 SSD (2TB) – Fast, reliable external storage
■ SanDisk Extreme Pro Portable SSD (1TB) – Compact and rugged
📌 Tip: Always backup your footage after every shoot.

● Protective Gear & Camera Bags
■ Lowepro ProTactic BP 450 AW II – Best backpack for carrying gear
■ Peak Design Everyday Sling 10L – Compact, stylish shoulder bag
■ Think Tank Airport Security V3.0 – Best for traveling photographers
📌 Tip: A rain cover protects your gear in bad weather.

■ Cleaning & Maintenance Kit
■ Rocket Blower – Removes dust from the sensor
■ Lens Cleaning Wipes – Prevents smudges on the lens
■ Sensor Cleaning Kit – Safely cleans image sensor
📌 Tip: Clean your lens and sensor regularly to avoid dust spots in images.

The right lenses and accessories will enhance your Canon EOS R5 Mark II experience, making photography and videography easier, more professional, and more enjoyable.
■ Invest in the right lenses based on your photography needs
■ Carry extra batteries and high-speed memory cards
■ Use a tripod or gimbal for stability
■ Improve audio quality with an external mio
■ Protect and maintain your Camera with cleaning kits and bags
In the next chapter, we'll discuss Maintenance, Troubleshooting, and Firmware Updates, ensuring your EOS R5 Mark II stays in top condition for years to come.

Maintenance, Troubleshooting, and Firmware Updates

Keeping your Canon EOS R5 Mark II in top condition ensures optimal performance and longevity. Proper maintenance, troubleshooting, and regular firmware updates help prevent malfunctions and keep your Camera up to date with new features and improvements.

In this chapter, we'll cover:

■ Cleaning and protecting your Camera and lenses

■ Common camera issues and troubleshooting solutions

■ Firmware updates – why they matter and how to install them

By the end, you'll know how to keep your Camera in excellent shape, avoid common issues, and ensure it runs smoothly for years to come.

Cleaning and Maintaining Your Camera

■ Cleaning the Camera Body

Dirt, dust, and moisture can accumulate on your Camera, leading to sticky buttons or sensor issues.

📌 How to Clean the Camera Body:

■ Use a soft microfiber cloth to wipe down the body.

■ For stubborn dirt, use a slightly damp cloth (avoid getting moisture into buttons or dials).

■ Keep the viewfinder and LCD screen clean with a lens cleaning wipe.

■ Tip: Store your Camera in a dry, dust-free place when not in use.

🔍 Cleaning the Lens Properly

A dirty lens can reduce image sharpness and cause lens flare.

📌 How to Clean the Lens:

■ Use a rocket blower to remove dust.

■ Gently wipe the lens glass with a microfiber cloth.

■ Use lens cleaning solution for smudges or fingerprints.

■ Always keep a UV filter on your lens for extra protection.

■ Tip: Never touch the lens glass directly with your fingers.

■ Cleaning the Image Sensor (Removing Dust Spots)

If you see dark spots in your images, dust may be on your camera sensor.

📌 How to Check for Sensor Dust:
⬛ Set the Camera to Manual Mode (M).
⬛ Use a small aperture (f/16 - f/22) and take a photo of a white wall or sky.
⬛ Review the image—if you see spots, the sensor needs cleaning.
📌 How to Clean the Sensor:
⬛ Use the Camera's Automatic Sensor Cleaning (Menu > Sensor Cleaning).
⬛ If dust remains, use a sensor cleaning swab and gentle strokes.
⬛ Avoid blowing air directly onto the sensor, as it may push dust further inside.
⬛ Tip: If you're uncomfortable cleaning the sensor, take it to a Canon Service Center.

🛡 Protecting Your Camera from Damage
⬛ Use a camera bag – Prevents dust, moisture, and physical damage.
⬛ Use a rain cover – Protects the Camera when shooting in bad weather.
⬛ Avoid extreme temperatures – Prolonged exposure to high heat or freezing cold can damage the battery and sensor.
⬛ Turn off the Camera before changing lenses – This reduces the chance of dust entering the sensor.
📌 Tip: Store your Camera with a silica gel pack to prevent moisture buildup in humid environments.

Troubleshooting Common Camera Issues

Even the best cameras encounter occasional issues. Here's how to fix the most common problems.
📌 Camera Won't Turn On
⬛ Check the battery – Ensure it's charged and inserted correctly.
⬛ Try another battery – Your current one may be faulty.
⬛ Check battery contacts – Clean with a dry cloth if dirty.
⬛ Remove memory cards and restart – Sometimes, a corrupt card causes issues.

Maintenance, Troubleshooting, and Firmware Updates

📌 Autofocus Not Working Properly

◼ Check AF/MF switch – Ensure your lens is set to AF (Autofocus).

◼ Select the correct AF mode – Some modes may not work with moving subjects.

◼ Clean the lens contacts – Dirty contacts can cause AF failure.

◼ Reset AF settings – (Menu > AF Settings > Reset to Default).

📌 Tip: Use One-Shot AF for still subjects and AI Servo AF for moving subjects.

📌 Memory Card Errors

◼ Use a high-speed card – Some cheap or slow cards won't work properly.

◼ Format the card in the Camera – (Menu > Format Card).

◼ Try another card – Your current card may be corrupted.

📌 Tip: Always format new cards in-camera instead of using a computer.

📌 Overheating Warning (Especially in 8K/4K Video)

◼ Reduce recording resolution – Use 4K Standard instead of 8K.

◼ Take breaks between shots – Allow the Camera to cool down.

◼ Turn off the LCD screen – Helps reduce heat buildup.

◼ Use an external recorder – Recording externally reduces internal heat.

📌 Tip: If shooting long videos, record in a cool environment and avoid direct sunlight.

📌 Camera Freezes or Becomes Unresponsive

◼ Remove the battery for 10 seconds, then restart.

◼ Update the firmware (Menu > Firmware Version > Update).

◼ Reset all settings (Menu > Reset Camera).

📌 Tip: Always use official Canon accessories to avoid compatibility issues.

Firmware Updates – Why They Matter & How to Install Them

Canon releases firmware updates to:

◼ Fix bugs and improve stability

◼ Enhance autofocus and image processing

◼ Add new features (e.g., improved video performance, new AF modes)

📌 How to Check and Update Firmware on the EOS R5 Mark II

◼ Go to Menu > Firmware Version and check the current version.

◼ Visit Canon's official website and download the latest firmware for the EOS R5 Mark II.

◼ Copy the firmware file to a formatted SD or CFexpress card.

◼ Insert the card into the Camera.

◼ Go to Menu > Firmware Update > Select the Update File.

◼ Follow the on-screen instructions.

◼ Tip: Keep the battery fully charged before updating to prevent failure.

When to Seek Professional Service

If your Camera has serious issues that you can't fix, contact Canon support or visit an authorized service center.

📌 Seek professional service if:

✗ The Camera doesn't turn on despite troubleshooting.

✗ Autofocus issues persist even after resetting settings.

✗ Sensor dust or spots don't clear after cleaning.

✗ The Camera overheats frequently, even at lower resolutions.

◼ Tip: Register your Camera with Canon's official warranty for repair benefits.

Proper maintenance, troubleshooting, and firmware updates will keep your Canon EOS R5 Mark II running smoothly and extend its lifespan.

◼ Clean your Camera and lenses regularly to prevent dust buildup.

◼ Troubleshoot common issues before seeking repairs.

◼ Keep firmware updated to benefit from the latest improvements.

Practical Photography Tips and Techniques

Mastering the Canon EOS R5 Mark II requires more than just knowing its settings—you need to apply practical techniques to capture stunning, high-quality images. Whether you're shooting portraits, landscapes, sports, or wildlife, these techniques will elevate your photography skills and make the most of your Camera's advanced features.

In this chapter, we'll cover:

- ◼ Composing the perfect shot
- ◼ Lighting techniques for stunning images
- ◼ Best camera settings for different scenarios
- ◼ Creative photography techniques
- ◼ Post-processing tips for a professional finish

By the end of this chapter, you'll have a toolbox of photography skills to consistently capture amazing photos.

Mastering Composition – How to Frame the Perfect Shot

Even with the best Camera, a poorly composed image won't look professional. Follow these composition techniques to create visually compelling photos.

📌 Rule of Thirds – The Foundation of Great Photography
- Imagine your image divided into a 3x3 grid.
- Place your subject at one of the four intersections rather than the center.
- This creates a balanced and natural-looking composition.

◼ Best for: Portraits, landscapes, and street photography.

📌 Tip: Enable the grid overlay in the camera menu for easier composition.

📌 Leading Lines – Guiding the Viewer's Eye
- Use natural lines (roads, rivers, fences) to draw attention to the subject.
- Creates depth and perspective in your images.

◼ Best for: Architecture, landscapes, and storytelling shots.

📌 Framing – Using Objects to Create depth
- Frame your subject using doorways, windows, trees, or arches.
- Adds a 3D effect and makes images more engaging.

◼ Best for: Street photography, travel shots, and portraits.

Practical Photography Tips and Techniques

📌 Symmetry & Reflections – Captivating Balanced Images
- Look for mirrored reflections in water or perfectly symmetrical scenes.
- Works well in architecture and nature photography.

■ Best for: Minimalist and artistic shots.

📌 Tip: Use a wide-angle lens (RF 15-35mm f/2.8) for architectural symmetry.

Lighting Techniques – Getting Perfect Exposure

Lighting is one of the most critical elements in photography. The EOS R5 Mark II's high dynamic range (HDR) sensor helps, but you still need to control light effectively.

📌 Golden Hour – The Best Natural Light
- Shoot during sunrise (6 AM - 8 AM) or sunset (5 PM - 7 PM) for soft, golden light.
- Avoid harsh midday sun, which creates strong shadows.

■ Best for: Portraits, landscapes, and outdoor photography.

📌 Tip: Use a reflector to bounce light onto your subject's face.

📌 Using Artificial Light for Indoor Shots
- Softbox or diffused LED lights provide natural-looking results.
- Avoid using the built-in camera flash—it creates harsh shadows.

■ Best for: Studio portraits and product photography.

📌 Tip: Use an external flash (Canon Speedlite 600EX II-RT) for controlled lighting.

📌 Using Shadows for Dramatic Effect
- Place light at an angle to create contrast and texture.
- Works well for moody portraits and black-and-white photography.

■ Best for: Artistic and cinematic photography.

📌 Tip: Adjust highlight and shadow levels in post-processing for the best results.

Best Camera Settings for Different Scenarios

The Canon EOS R5 Mark II is versatile, but each type of photography requires different settings. Here's how to adjust your Camera for the best results.

Practical Photography Tips and Techniques

■ Portrait Photography Settings
■ Aperture: f/1.8 – f/2.8 (blurry background)
■ Shutter Speed: 1/200s – 1/400s
■ ISO: 100 – 400 (depending on light)
■ Focus Mode: Eye Detection AF
📌 Tip: Use a prime lens (RF 85mm f/1.2) for the best bokeh.

■ Landscape Photography Settings
■ Aperture: f/8 – f/16 (sharp details)
■ Shutter Speed: 1/50s – 1/100s (for handheld), slower with a tripod
■ ISO: 100 – 200
■ Focus Mode: One-Shot AF
📌 Tip: Use a polarizing filter to reduce glare and enhance colors.

🏃 Sports & Action Photography Settings
■ Aperture: f/2.8 – f/5.6 (sharp subject, blurred background)
■ Shutter Speed: 1/1000s or faster
■ ISO: Auto (Max 3200)
■ Focus Mode: AI Servo AF (Tracking Mode)
📌 Tip: Use burst mode (30 fps) to capture fast-moving action.

🌙 Low Light & Night Photography Settings
■ Aperture: f/1.8 – f/2.8 (maximum light intake)
■ Shutter Speed: 1/15s – 30s (long exposures)
■ ISO: 800 – 6400 (balance brightness & noise)
■ Focus Mode: Manual Focus (Autofocus struggles in darkness)
📌 Tip: Use a tripod and shoot in RAW format for better noise reduction in post-processing.

■ Street Photography Settings
■ Aperture: f/5.6 – f/8 (balanced depth of field)
■ Shutter Speed: 1/250s – 1/500s
■ ISO: 200 – 1600
■ Focus Mode: Zone AF or Spot AF
📌 Tip: Use silent shutter mode for candid shots.

Practical Photography Tips and Techniques

Creative Photography Techniques

📌 Long Exposure Photography (Smooth Water & Light Trails)
- Use a slow shutter speed (5s – 30s) for waterfalls and city lights.
- Use a tripod to avoid blur.

📌 Tip: Use an ND filter in daylight to prevent overexposure.

📌 Panning Photography (Motion Blur for Action Shots)
- Set shutter speed to 1/30s – 1/60s.
- Follow the moving subject with the Camera while pressing the shutter.

📌 Best for: Racing cars, cyclists, running athletes.

📌 Black & White Photography for Dramatic Images
- Use Monochrome Picture Style in-camera.
- Adjust contrast and shadows in post-processing for depth.

📌 Tip: Works great in portraits and street photography.

Post-Processing Tips for a Professional Look

Even with perfect settings, editing enhances your final image.

■ Lightroom & Photoshop – Best for color grading and retouching.

■ Increase sharpness and contrast to enhance details.

■ Use the Healing Brush to remove distractions.

■ Adjust shadows and highlights for better dynamic range.

📌 Tip: Always shoot in RAW format for more editing flexibility

The Canon EOS R5 Mark II is a powerful camera, but knowing the right techniques will help you capture stunning photos every time.

■ Use strong compositions like the Rule of Thirds

■ Master lighting for perfect exposure

■ Adjust camera settings based on the scene

■ Try creative techniques to stand out

■ Edit your images for a polished, professional look